A Little Book of
Irish Baking

Marion Maxwell
Illustrated by
Catherine McWilliams

First published in 1996 by
Appletree Press Ltd.
The Old Potato Station
14 Howard Street South
Belfast BT7 1AP
Tel: +44 (0) 28 90 243074
Fax: +44 (0) 28 90 246756
E-mail: frontdesk@appletree.ie
Web Site: www.appletree.ie

A Little Book of Irish Baking

A catalogue record for this book is
available from The British Library.

ISBN 0-86281-534-7

9 8 7 6 5 4 3

A Little Book of Irish Baking

Just as it was thought in the old days that the fire should never be allowed to go out, so the baking of breads and cakes has always been central to our traditions of home and hearth. Happily, home baking skills are still flourishing, thanks to the pride we take in being known for our ready hospitality. This little book charts our baking repertoire from the oatcakes and soda breads that were for so long an essential part of the staple diet, to richer fare that includes festive specialities, up-to-date favourites and cherished family recipes that have stood the test of time.

Boxty

Boxty on the griddle
Boxty on the pan
If you can't make boxty
You'll never get a man

A friend of mine takes the work out of this by spinning the raw potatoes in a cloth in her washing machine! Boxty can also be baked as a cake or formed into "hurleys" and boiled. Though it is not traditional, some people add melted butter to the mashed potato to give a shorter mixture.

450g/1lb raw potatoes, peeled and grated
450g/1lb cooked potatoes, mashed
450g/1lb plain flour
2 tsp salt
1 tsp baking soda

Makes 4.
Put the grated potato on a linen cloth and wring tightly, catching all the liquid in a bowl. Mix grated and mashed potatoes together. Add the starch sediment that will have settled at the bottom of the collected liquid. Sift flour, salt and baking soda and mix well with the potato. Knead the mixture, shape into a circle and cut into "farls" or quarters. Cook on a hot griddle. Serve immediately spread with butter or reheat later by frying the farls with bacon.

Oatcakes

Oats are one of our oldest native crops. These unleavened cakes, also known as **strones** in Ulster and **bannocks** in Scotland, were traditionally eaten spread with butter. They were baked on the griddle, then dried out on ornamental "harnen" stands. Delicious with cheese or honey.

25g/1oz plain flour
pinch salt
pinch baking soda
110g/4oz medium oatmeal

25g/1oz butter, margarine or bacon fat
¼ cup boiling water

Makes 4.

Sift the flour, salt and baking soda into the oatmeal. Melt the butter, margarine or fat in boiling water and add to the dry ingredients. Mix until the mixture is a spongy mass (a little extra water can be used if necessary). Turn mixture on to a surface covered with plenty of dry oatmeal and scatter more on top. Flatten the dough and roll out until ½ cm/ ¼ inch in thickness, then place a dinner plate on top and trim into a neat circle. Scatter on more oatmeal and rub it in all over the surface. Cut into quarters before baking on either a griddle or in the oven.

Griddle method: Place the oatcakes on a heated griddle or heavy pan over medium heat and bake until they dry out and curl. Then place under a grill at medium heat to cook the top of the oatcakes.

Oven method: Bake at gas mark 4, 180°C, 350°F, for 20-30 minutes or until dried out.

Potato Apple Cake

If you are trying this for the first time, you will soon realise
why it has long been considered the highlight of a farm-
house tea. Be sure to cook it until the apples are soft and
don't stint on the sugar and butter which melt into a delicious sauce at the end. Traditionally, at Hallowe'en, a ring
would be hidden in the filling for luck.

1 batch potato bread dough (see p.31)
275g/10oz Bramley apples, peeled and thinly sliced
butter and sugar to taste

Makes 2.
Divide the potato dough in two and roll each half into a
circle about 20cm/8 inch in diameter. Arrange the apples
on half of each circle, then fold over to form pastie shapes
and crimp around the edges to give a good seal. Cook as
for potato bread in a heavy pan or on the griddle, turning
half-way through. Brown slowly to ensure that the apples
have time to soften, approximately 20 minutes. Gently slit
open the cakes and insert slivers of butter and plenty of
sugar. Reseal and return to heat for 5 minutes, to allow the
sauce to form.

Yeast Bread With Stout

This is my version of the time-honoured beer bread, made in celebration of stout - the dark brew that has become associated the world over with Ireland. The recipe is failsafe, ideal for those not too familiar with yeast cookery.

1 tbsp (heaped) soft brown sugar
275ml/10fl oz stout
50g/2oz butter
25g/1oz fresh yeast
1 tsp (level) salt
1 egg, beaten

225g/8oz wholemeal flour
225g/8oz strong white flour
1 tsp ground ginger (optional)
1 tsp caraway seeds (optional)

Preheat oven to gas mark 5, 190°C, 375°F, and grease a 900g/2lb loaf tin. Place sugar, stout and butter in a large saucepan and bring to boil, then cool until lukewarm. Add a spoonful of this liquid to the yeast and mix until creamy. Add yeast, salt and egg to the stout mixture. Sift flour into a large, warmed, mixing bowl, with ginger and caraway seeds. Make a well in the centre of the dry ingredients and add liquid. Mix with a knife, then your fingers until it forms a soft dough. Knead for 10 minutes until smooth, elastic, and a little shiny. Return dough to bowl and cover with oiled clingfilm. Leave in a warm place until the dough has doubled in size. Then knead again until smooth, put in loaf tin, cover and set aside to prove a second time. When dough has doubled in bulk again, put in oven and bake for about 35 minutes. Bread is ready if it sounds hollow when tapped.

A Trio Of Breads For Tea

These three favourites, all enriched forms of basic soda bread, often appear together on the tea table. In each case use the recipe for soda bread (p. 32) plus the extras listed below.

Currant Soda

50g/2oz caster sugar
25g/1oz butter or margarine

175g/6oz dried fruit
1 egg, beaten (optional)

Add sugar to soda bread dry ingredients and rub in butter or margarine. Stir in fruit. Add beaten egg, if using, to buttermilk and proceed as for soda bread.

Treacle Bread

50g/2oz caster sugar
50g/2oz butter or margarine
50g/2oz sultanas (optional)

2 tbsp treacle
1 egg, beaten
pinch ginger (optional)

Add sugar to soda bread dry ingredients and rub in butter or margarine. Stir in fruit if using. Add treacle, egg and ginger to buttermilk and proceed as for soda bread.

Cornmeal Bread

Cornmeal, known as "yalla male" or "india buck", was first imported into Ireland during the Great Famine. Simply use half coarse cornmeal and half plain flour in the basic soda bread recipe.

Flakemeal Crunchies

This is an updated version of the ever-popular oat biscuits. The coating of demerara sugar, adds a special crunch and is an inspired touch.

175g/6oz flour
1 tsp baking soda
1 tsp baking powder
175g/6oz caster sugar
110g/4oz butter
110g/4oz white pastry fat
1 egg

110g/4oz rolled oats (flake meal)
50g/2oz Weetabix, crushed
50g/2oz cornflakes, roughly crushed
50g/2oz coconut
80g/3oz demerara sugar

Makes 30.
Preheat oven to gas mark 4, 180°C, 350°F, and grease two baking trays. Sift flour, baking soda and baking powder together. Cream together caster sugar, butter and pastry fat. Add egg and mix well, then fold in flour mixture, cereals and coconut. Shape into balls the size of a large walnut and roll each in demerara sugar. Flatten into rounds, place on baking trays and bake for 20-25 minutes until golden brown.

Currant Squares

Even in the age of convenience foods, home baking skills are flourishing, though the preference has shifted from large cakes to tray bakes. Here is an unsurpassed favourite, especially when made with a delicate flaky pastry.

Flaky Pastry:
140g/5oz firm butter or margarine, grated
175g/6oz flour
pinch salt
iced water

Filling:
110g/4oz butter
80g/3oz sugar
225g/8oz currants
pinch spice
1 lemon, rind and juice
1 large apple, grated
1 slice bread, crumbled

Makes 20.

To make pastry: freeze butter or margarine for half an hour before grating. Sift flour and salt, then add butter or margarine and, using a palette knife, mix into flour. Add iced water until a dough is formed. Wrap and chill in fridge. Put all filling ingredients in a saucepan and bring to boiling point. Set aside to cool. Preheat oven to gas mark 6, 200°C, 400°F. Roll out half the pastry very thinly and line a swiss roll tin. Pour on currant filling, spreading evenly, then cover with the rest of the pastry. Glaze with egg or milk and bake for 30 minutes or until light gold in colour. Dust with caster sugar and cut into squares when cool.

Kerry Apple Cake

This cake does not keep very well, but that is not usually a problem, as you can be sure it will disappear very quickly! It is best eaten warm with cream or Greek-style yoghurt, and it is also perfect with cheese.

175g/6oz butter
175g/6oz caster sugar
2 eggs, beaten
225g/8oz self-raising flour
2 medium cooking apples, peeled, cored and chopped

1 tsp lemon rind
2 tbsp demerara sugar
pinch cinnamon
pinch nutmeg

Preheat oven to gas mark 4, 180°C, 350°F, and grease and line a 900g/2lb loaf tin. Cream butter and sugar. Gradually add eggs and flour. Stir in apples and lemon rind. Pour into the tin and sprinkle with sugar and spices. Bake for 1-1½ hours.

Whiskey Tea Brack

Tea brack derives its moisture and flavour from the strong, sweet tea in which the fruit is soaked overnight. This is my version of a recipe given to the late Theodora Fitzgibbon by her grandmother who soaked the fruit in a mixture of half tea and half whiskey!

225g/8oz sultanas
225g/8oz raisins
225g/8oz soft brown sugar
½ tsp cinnamon
¼ tsp grated nutmeg
2 tbsp whiskey

275ml/10fl oz strong tea
450g/1lb self-raising flour
2 eggs, beaten
marmalade or honey to glaze
demerara sugar to dust

Place the sultanas, raisins, sugar, cinnamon, nutmeg, whiskey and tea in a large bowl and soak overnight. Preheat oven to gas mark 3, 160°C, 325°F, and grease and line a 20cm/8 inch round cake tin. Stir in the sieved flour and eggs and mix well. Bake for approximately 1½ hours. Towards the end of baking time, brush with marmalade or honey and sprinkle with demerara sugar. To test if the brack is cooked insert a skewer into the centre, if it comes out clean then the brack is ready. When cold, slice and butter generously.

Wheaten Bread

Ask Irish emigrés what they miss about home and it's likely they will name wheaten bread as one of the things they hanker for. Conventionally, it is a variant on white soda bread made with half wholemeal flour, but this version uses all wholemeal enriched with wheatgerm, bran and oats. It needs no kneading, slices well and is delicious with smoked salmon, cheese or honey.

110g/4oz plain white flour
3 tsp (level) baking soda
½ to ¼ tsp salt
275g/10oz coarse wholemeal flour
275g/10oz fine wholemeal flour
2 tbsp wheatgerm

80g/3oz pinhead or rolled oats
2 tbsp bran
1 tbsp (scant) brown sugar
50g/2oz butter, margarine (or 2-2½ tbsp olive oil)
825ml/1½ pt buttermilk

Preheat oven to gas mark 6, 200°C, 400°F, and grease and flour two 900g/2lb loaf tins. Sieve plain flour with baking soda and salt. Stir in other dry ingredients and rub in butter or margarine (or stir in the olive oil.) Gradually add the buttermilk until the mixture is slack enough to spoon into the tins. Place in the oven and bake for 50-60 minutes. To test if the wheaten is cooked through, tap on the bottom, if it sounds hollow it is ready. Cover with a cloth until cold. This bread freezes well.

Buttermilk Scones

Morning coffee and afternoon tea would not be complete without fresh scones and there are so many delicious varieties. The secret of making good scones is a quick, light hand when mixing and a hot oven.

225g/8oz self-raising soda-bread flour
pinch salt
25g/1oz butter or hard margarine

1 egg, beaten
140ml/5fl oz buttermilk
egg or milk to glaze (optional)

Makes 8.

Preheat oven to gas mark 8, 230°C, 450°F. Sift flour with salt and rub in butter or margarine. Make a well in the centre and pour in the egg and most of the buttermilk. Mix quickly to form a soft dough, adding a little extra buttermilk if necessary. Turn out on to a floured surface and roll out lightly until 2.5cm/1 inch in thickness. Working quickly, cut into 5cm/2 inch rounds. Glaze with egg or milk and set on a floured baking sheet. Bake for 15-20 minutes until light brown.

Savoury Cheese and Herb Scones

Add 1 tsp dry mustard, 50g (2oz) grated cheese and 2 tbsp fresh, chopped herbs to the dry ingredients and proceed as before. After brushing with egg or milk, scatter a little grated cheese on the top of each scone.

Wheaten Scones

These are staple fare in my home, eaten with butter and honey. Many versions use half white flour but all wholemeal makes for a nuttier scone, further enhanced by the use of molasses-rich sugar.

450g/1lb coarse wholemeal flour	*80g/3oz dark muscovado sugar*
pinch salt	*50g/2oz butter or margarine*
1 tsp (heaped) baking soda	
1 tsp (heaped) cream of tartar	*2 eggs, beaten*
	175ml/6fl oz buttermilk

Makes 8.

Preheat oven to gas mark 8, 220°C, 450°F, and grease a baking sheet. Sieve flour with salt, baking soda and cream of tartar, returning the bran left in the sieve to the flour. Rub in sugar and fat and make a well in the middle of the dry mixture. Add the eggs and most of the buttermilk, incorporating it quickly and lightly and adding extra, if necessary, to form a soft dough. Roll out on a floured surface until 2.5cm/1 inch in thickness, cut into rounds about 5cm/2 inch in diameter. Place on a greased baking sheet and bake for 15-20 minutes.

Date Scones

For this delicious variation, use 175g/6oz white flour and 340g/12oz wholemeal flour, and add 110g/4oz chopped dates to the dry ingredients.

Scripture Cake

This delicious fruit cake is perfect for Sunday tea and for entertaining visitors. The recipe is cleverly devised to send you thumbing through your bible to decipher the ingredients. The results, of course, are divine!

110g/4oz Jeremiah Ch. I v. 11
340g/12oz Jeremiah Ch. XXIV v. 2
340g/12oz I Chronicles Ch. XII v. 40
500g/1lb 2oz Leviticus Ch. II v. 2
2 tsp (level) Galacians Ch. V v. 9
1 tsp (level) Solomon Ch. IV v. 14
pinch St. Matthew Ch.V v. 13
6 Job Ch.XXXIX v. 14
340g/12oz Isaiah Ch. VII v. 15
450g/1lb Jeremiah Ch. VI v. 20
½ breakfast cup Solomon Ch. IV v. 11
2 tbsp I Samuel Ch. XIV v. 29

Preheat oven to gas mark 3, 180°C, 350°F, and grease and line a 22cm/9 inch cake tin. Blanch, peel and chop the almonds. Chop the figs. Sift flour with baking powder, cinnamon and salt. Cream butter and caster sugar until fluffy. Gradually mix in beaten eggs, adding a little flour with each addition. Fold in the rest of the flour along with the honey, milk and fruit. Turn into tin and bake for approximately 2¼ hours. The cake is ready when a skewer is inserted and comes out clean.

Potato Bread

Also known as **fadge** or **potato cake**, this is delicious hot from the griddle or pan with melted butter and a sprinkling of sugar. It is also a much loved part of a traditional fried breakfast.

225g/8oz warm cooked potato
½ tsp salt
25g/1oz butter, melted
50g/2oz plain flour

Makes 8.
Mash potatoes well. Add salt and butter, then work in enough flour to make a pliable dough. Divide the dough in two and roll out on a floured surface to form two circles 22cm/9 inch in diameter and ½cm/¼ inch in thickness. Cut each circle into quarters and bake on a hot griddle or pan for about 5 minutes or until browned on both sides. Some people like to grease the baking surface, while others prefer a light dusting of flour for a drier effect.

Pratie Oaten

For a tasty, textured variation substitute fine oatmeal for the flour in the recipe above.

Soda Bread

When white flour became widely available, this bread became the mainstay of daily baking in Ireland - and there is still no better way to set off the taste of home-made jam. A friend of mine still makes soda bread in a bastable pot oven inside her gas cooker, but I have found that a heavy cast-iron casserole dish with a lid is equally effective. This bread rises up beautifully and the crust is well-formed but not hard.

450g/1lb plain white flour
1 tsp (heaped) baking soda
1 tsp salt
340-400ml/12-14fl oz buttermilk

Preheat oven to gas mark 6, 200°C, 400°F, and warm a 18cm/7 inch cast-iron, lidded casserole dish. Sift dry ingredients into a large mixing bowl, make a well in the centre and gradually add the buttermilk until all the flour has been incorporated. Turn the dough out on to a floured surface and knead lightly, then form into a smooth round. Dust the inside of the casserole dish with flour and place the dough inside. Score a deep cross into the top of the dough. Cover and bake for approximately 50-55 minutes or until the bottom sounds hollow when tapped. Turn out and wrap in a cloth until cold.

Soda Farls

Before the advent of the bastable oven or the range, most bread was baked on a griddle, swung over the fire or set on a trivet. Rolled thin for ease of baking, griddle bread is traditionally cut in four "farls" or quarters. The soda farl has remained popular, not least as part of an Ulster Fry. If you don't have a griddle, a heavy frying pan or an electric pan will do equally well.

Makes 4.
Make a batch of soda bread dough (p. 32) and roll out on a floured surface to form a circle 2.5cm/1 inch in thickness. Cut the circle into quarters and bake on a griddle or in the oven.

Griddle method: Place the farls on a moderately hot griddle and cook slowly over a gentle heat until they have risen and a white skin has formed on top, approximately 5-8 minutes. Turn over and cook underside until browned. When cooked the farls will sound hollow if tapped.

Oven method: Preheat oven to gas mark 6, 200°C, 400° F. Place farls on a preheated baking tray and bake for 40-45 minutes.

Seed Cake

For centuries, caraway seeds have been used to lend a distinctive flavour to puddings, biscuits and cakes. A handful would often be thrown in to speckle a sweetened soda bread. This rich cake, known also as "carvie", recalls days of gracious living in substantial country houses, when visiting ladies would be offered a slice with a glass of port.

275g/10oz flour	225g/8oz butter
½ tsp baking powder	225g/8oz caster sugar
¼ tsp cinnamon	4 eggs, beaten
¼ tsp nutmeg	3 tbsp caraway seeds

Preheat oven to gas mark 3, 160°C, 325°F, and grease and line a 20cm/8 inch cake tin. Sift flour with baking powder, cinnamon and nutmeg. In a separate bowl, cream the butter and sugar together until pale and fluffy, then gradually mix in the eggs, adding a little flour with each addition. Fold in the rest of the flour and mix well. Reserve a teaspoon of the caraway seeds to decorate the top of the cake and stir the rest into the mixture. Bake for approximately 1½ hours, until pale gold in colour and firm to the touch.

Lila's Apple Tart

This is how the best baker in my neighbourhood makes this universal family favourite. It combines the tartness of Bramleys, a couple of Cox's Pippins and, following the old books, a quince for superb flavour.

Shortcrust Pastry:
8oz/225g self raising flour
pinch salt
2oz/50g white pastry fat
2oz/50g good quality margarine
1 egg, beaten
Filling:
450g/1lb Bramley apples,
peeled, cored and thinly sliced
225g/8oz Cox's Pippins, peeled, cored and thinly sliced
1 quince, grated (optional)
3 tbsp (heaped) sugar
nutmeg or cloves, grated
caster sugar to dust

To make the pastry: Sift the flour and salt into a large mixing bowl. Cut the fat and margarine into small cubes and rub into the flour until the mixture resembles breadcrumbs. Mix the egg with a little water, reserve some to use as a glaze, and use the rest to bind the flour into a dough. Then wrap and chill in the fridge for 30 minutes. Preheat oven to gas mark 6, 200°C, 400°F, warm a baking sheet, and grease and line a 24cm/9 inch pie dish. Roll out a little more than half the pastry on a floured surface and line the pie dish. Place apples and quince (if using) into the dish and add sugar and a little freshly grated nutmeg or cloves. Roll out the rest of the pastry to form a lid. Brush the rim of the pastry base with water and place the lid on top. Seal and flute edges and make a few slits in the lid to allow steam to escape. Glaze with reserved egg and sprinkle with caster sugar. Place pie dish on the warmed baking sheet and bake for 30 minutes. Serve with cream.

Old Fashioned Ginger Cake

In ancient times, cakes flavoured with ginger, known as "craebh", were associated with Midsummer customs: a basket of cakes was placed on a pole and dancers would compete to win them.

110g/4oz butter or margarine
110g/4oz soft brown sugar
3 dsp golden syrup
3 dsp treacle
225g/8oz plain flour
1 tsp baking soda
1 tsp cinnamon
1½ tsp ground ginger
1 eggs
3 tbsp buttermilk
50g/2oz crystallised ginger, chopped (optional)

In a saucepan, gently melt the butter, sugar, golden syrup and treacle together, then set aside to cool. Preheat oven to gas mark 4, 180°C, 350°F, and grease and line a 20cm/8 inch cake tin. Sift flour, soda and spices. Beat egg with buttermilk and mix well into dry ingredients. Reserve a teaspoon of the chopped ginger to decorate, and add the rest to the dry ingredients. Pour into the cake tin and bake for approximately 1 hour. When the cake is cool decorate with orange glace icing and the reserved crystallised ginger.

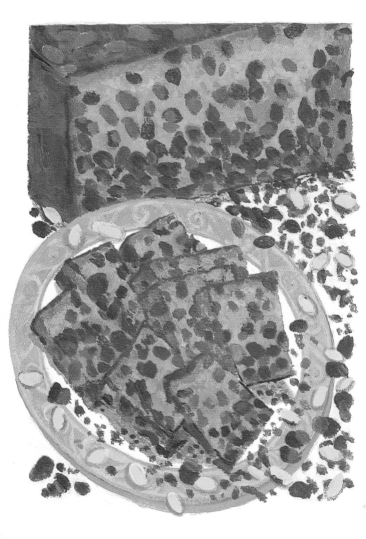

Porter Cake

When Arthur Guinness began brewing porter at St. James's Gate, Dublin in 1759, he could hardly have envisaged that his distinctive stout would become a household name.

275g/10oz plain flour
generous ½ tsp baking soda
2 tsp mixed spice
225g/8oz butter or margarine
225g/8oz soft brown sugar
4 eggs, beaten

225g/8oz raisins
225g/8oz sultanas
110g/4oz peel
110g/4oz walnuts, chopped
rind of 1 lemon, grated
5-6fl oz Guinness

Preheat oven to gas mark 3, 170°C, 325°F, and grease and line a 18cm/7 inch cake tin. Sift flour, baking soda and spice into a mixing bowl. In a separate bowl, cream the butter and sugar together until fluffy. Gradually beat in eggs, adding a little flour with each addition. Fold in the rest of the flour and stir in the fruit, peel, nuts and rind. Pour in half of the Guinness, mix well and pour into the cake tin. Bake for 1 hour then reduce the temperature to gas mark 2, 150°C, 300°F; cover cake lightly with grease-proof paper and bake for a further 1½ hours. To test if the cake is done insert a skewer; if it comes out clean the cake is ready. Remove from the oven and allow to cool before turning out of the tin. Prick the cake all over with a skewer or fork and drizzle the remaining Guinness over. Wrap in foil and store for a week before cutting.

Irish Chocolate Cake

The "Irishness" of this lovely chocolate cake is thanks not only to the wonderful liqueur used in the filling, but also to a certain, very Irish, ingredient in the cake mixture itself which contributes to its moistness.

Sponge:
175g/6oz self-raising flour
½ tsp salt
50g/2oz dark chocolate
110g/4oz butter
175g/6oz caster sugar
80g/3oz cooked mashed potato

2 eggs, beaten
4 tbsp milk
Filling:
110g/4oz dark chocolate
125ml/4fl oz double cream
50g/2oz icing sugar
3 tbsp Irish cream liqueur

Preheat oven to gas mark 5, 190°C, 375°F, and grease and line two 20cm/8 inch cake tins. Sift flour and salt into a mixing bowl. Melt chocolate in a bowl placed over a saucepan of hot water. In a separate bowl, cream butter and sugar together until fluffy, then beat in the chocolate and mashed potato. Gradually beat in the eggs, adding a little flour with each addition. Fold in the rest of the flour and stir in the milk. Divide mixture between cake tins and bake for 25-30 minutes or until top is firm but springy to the touch. Remove from oven and after a few minutes, turn out on to a cooling rack. While the cake is cooling make the filling. Melt the chocolate as before, stir in the other ingredients and mix well. Use the filling to sandwich the sponge layers together and coat the top and sides of the cake.

Dropped Scones

Add these airy little scones - also known as **Scottish pancakes** - to your baking repertoire and you'll never be lost for something to offer to unexpected guests. Ready in minutes, they are delicious spread with lemon curd.

110g/4oz self-raising flour
½ tsp baking powder
1 dsp sugar
1 tbsp melted butter or cooking oil
1 egg, beaten
175ml/6 fl oz milk

Makes 10.
Sift flour and baking powder into a large mixing bowl. Add the sugar and stir in the butter or oil, egg and most of the milk, and mix well. Add the remaining milk until the mixture is a thick, smooth batter able to hold its shape when dropped in little rounds on a griddle or pan. When bubbles appear on the surface turn over and cook the other side. (It is a good idea to make a trial scone to test the temperature of the griddle.) When cooked, the scones should be golden brown and spongy inside.

Country Rhubarb Cake

Both my parents ate this as children, dished straight out of the pot oven. The fruit and sugar would boil out around the sides, resulting in the gooey, syrupy cake they remember as a heavenly treat. The scone dough is quicker to make than pastry and absorbs the lovely juices better.

Scone dough:
340g/12oz *plain flour*
½ tsp *baking soda*
pinch salt
50g/2oz *caster sugar*
80g/3oz *butter*
1 *egg*

175ml/6fl oz *buttermilk*
Filling:
700g/1½lb *rhubarb,*
roughly chopped
200-250g/7-9oz *sugar*
white of 1 egg, whisked
caster sugar to dust

Preheat oven to gas mark 4, 180°C, 350°F, and grease a 25cm/10 inch deep pie dish. Sieve flour, baking soda and salt into a mixing bowl. Add caster sugar and rub in butter. In a separate bowl, beat the egg together with the buttermilk and gradually add this to the flour until a dough is formed. Knead lightly on a floured surface and divide dough into two. Roll out one half and use it to line the pie dish. Fill the dish with the rhubarb and sprinkle with the sugar. Roll out the remaining dough to form a pastry lid. Brush the rim of the pastry base with water and put on the lid. Glaze with the whisked egg white and sprinkle with caster sugar. Make steam slits in the lid and bake for 50-60 minutes or until the crust is lightly browned and the fruit is soft. This pie is also delicious if made with apples.

Barmbrack

"Barm" derives either from *bairm* - an early form of ale yeast - or *bairin* meaning cake, while "brack" comes from the Irish *breac* meaning spotted.

25g/1oz fresh yeast	½ tsp salt
80g/3oz caster sugar	2oz/50g butter
275ml/10fl oz tepid milk	225g/8oz sultanas
1 egg, beaten	110g/4oz currants
450g/1lb strong white flour	50g/2oz mixed peel
½ tsp cinnamon	2 tbsp sugar dissolved in
¼ tsp grated nutmeg	2 tbsp hot water to glaze

Cream together the yeast and 1 teaspoon each of the sugar and milk. Mix well then add the remaining milk and the egg. Sieve flour, spices and salt into a mixing bowl, rub in the butter and add the fruit and peel. Stir in the yeast mixture and beat well with a wooden spoon then, using your hands, form a dough and knead on a floured surface for 10 minutes until the dough becomes elastic. Place in a greased bowl, cover with oiled polythene and leave in a warm place for about an hour. Divide dough in half and knead each for a few minutes, then place each in a cake tin and return to a warm place for another hour until well risen. Preheat oven to gas mark 6, 200°C, 400°F. Bake for 30-35 minutes then remove from heat. Dissolve sugar in hot water and glaze while hot.

Lemon and Vanilla Curd Cake

Curds were once an important part of the Irish diet, and were also useful for paying the rent. Recipes for this delicately flavoured cheesecake are found in several eighteenth century "receipt" books.

175g/6oz sweet shortcrust pastry
Filling:
40g/1½ butter
50g/2oz vanilla flavoured sugar (or caster sugar plus essence)
2 egg yolks
1 tbsp (heaped) plain flour

rind and juice of ½ lemon
225g/8oz cottage cheese
Topping:
1 tbsp flour
1 tbsp sugar
1 tbsp butter, melted
1 egg, beaten
caster sugar to dust

Preheat oven to gas mark 4, 180°C, 350°F, warm a baking sheet and grease a loose-bottomed flan tin. Roll out the shortcrust pastry until thin, then line the flan tin with the dough, trimming off any excess. Chill pastry case in the fridge. Cream the butter and sugar together until fluffy, then beat in the egg yolks, flour, lemon rind, lemon juice and sieved cottage cheese. Mix well, then spoon into the pastry case. Mix topping ingredients together and spread on top of the curd filling. Place the flan tin on the warmed baking sheet and bake for approximately 1 hour or until the top is lightly browned and slightly firm. Dust with caster sugar and serve cool but not chilled.

Buttermilk Pancakes

Cooked on the griddle or the pan, these are traditional fare for Shrove Tuesday as they use eggs, milk and butter, all of which were forbidden during a strict Lenten fast.

225g/8oz plain flour
1 tsp baking soda
½ tsp salt
1 tbsp caster sugar
1 egg, beaten
275ml/10 fl oz buttermilk

Makes 10.
Sieve dry ingredients into a bowl and add the egg. Add buttermilk gradually until the mixture is a thick, creamy consistency. Spoon on to a hot, greased griddle and cook gently until golden. Flip over and brown the other side. Serve hot, spread with butter and sprinkled with sugar.

Nessie's Boiled Fruit Cake

With the main ingredients quickly measured out in cupfuls (a standard breakfast cup will do) and no creaming or rubbing-in to be done, this cut-and-come-again cake is an established favourite. Delicious sliced and buttered for tea. My version is named after a lovely lady and a great baker whose recipes were much sought after.

1 cup water	1¼ cups sultanas
225g/8oz butter	¼ cup cherries
1 cup soft brown sugar	1 tsp mixed spice
½ cup peel	2 cups flour
1½ cups raisins	1 tsp baking soda
	2 eggs, beaten

Put first eight ingredients into a large saucepan and bring to a boil. Simmer gently for 20 minutes, then set aside to cool. Preheat oven to gas mark 4, 180°C, 350°F, and grease and line a 20cm/8 inch cake tin. Sieve the flour and baking soda into the fruit mixture and add the beaten eggs. Mix well, then turn into a cake tin and bake for 1-1½ hours or until cooked through. (Reduce the temperature towards the end of the cooking time if necessary.) Cool in the tin for 15 minutes, then turn out on to a rack. This cake will keep well if stored in an airtight tin.

Featherlight Sponge Cake

This light-as-air cake is often used as a yardstick for judging the best baker in the parish, some of whom will swear by using duck eggs for extra volume. Perfect simply sandwiched with jam and cream, this basic mixture can also be transformed into a swiss roll, a layered gateau or a trifle base.

4 large eggs, separated
4oz/110g caster sugar
4oz/110g self-raising flour, sieved

Preheat oven to gas mark 4, 180°C, 350°F, and grease and line two 18cm/7 inch cake tins. Beat egg yolks and sugar together until very pale and thick, then set aside. In a separate bowl, beat the egg whites until they stand in stiff peaks. Fold the egg whites into the egg and sugar mixture, then gently fold in the flour. Divide the mixture between the cake tins and bake in the middle of the oven for about 25-30 minutes, until the sponge has shrunk slightly from the sides of the tins and is firm and springy to the touch. When cold, sandwich together with jam, cream, fresh fruit, lemon curd or a combination of these. Finish with a dusting of caster sugar, or make a pretty pattern by sprinkling icing sugar over a doily set on the cake.

Index

Apple Tart, Lila's 39

Bannocks 7
Barmbrack 51
Boiled Fruit Cake, Nessie's 56
Boxty 4
Buttermilk Pancakes 55
Buttermilk Scones 24

Cheese and Herb Scones,
  Savoury 24
Chocolate Cake, Irish 44
Cornmeal Bread 12
Country Rhubarb Cake 48
Curd Cake, Lemon and Vanilla 52
Currant Soda Bread 12
Currant Squares 16

Date Scones 27
Dropped Scones 47

Fadge 31
Featherlight Sponge Cake 59
Flakemeal Crunchies 15
Fruit Cake, Nessie's Boiled 56

Ginger Cake, Old Fashioned 40

Irish Chocolate Cake 44

Kerry Apple Cake 19

Lemon and Vanilla Curd Cake 52
Lila's Apple Tart 39

Nessie's Boiled Fruit Cake 56

Oatcakes 7
Old Fashioned Ginger Cake 40

Pancakes, Buttermilk 55
Porter Cake 43
Potato Apple Cake 8
Potato Bread 31
Potato Cake 31
Pratie Oaten 31

Rhubarb Cake, Country 48

Savoury Cheese and Herb Scones 24
Scones, Buttermilk 24
Scones, Date 27
Scones, Savoury Cheese and Herb 24
Scones, Wheaten 27
Scottish Pancakes 47
Scripture Cake 28
Seed Cake 36
Soda Bread 32
Soda Farls 35
Sponge Cake, Featherlight 59
Strones 7

Teabreads 12
Treacle Bread 12

Wheaten Bread 23
Wheaten Scones 27
Whiskey Tea Brack 20

Yeast Bread with Stout 11